Saints for Communities
ACTIVITY BOOK

- For ages 4-9
- Reproducible pages are formatted for easy copying

Jeff Albrecht

Saints · FOR · COMMUNITIES
Saints AND me!

Liguori

Acknowledgments

I extend my thanks to Barbara Yoffie for creating these friendly, wonderful stories that draw children closer to God. I also thank Julia DiSalvo, my editor at Liguori Publications, for developing these concepts and activities with me. Her direction and guidance helped put the entire *Saints for Communities* set together.

HIDDEN OBJECTS

This Lasallian teacher is missing a few school supplies.
Circle the items listed.

app
gl
bo
ru
chalkboa
eras
eyeglass
pai
brush
tissue b

SPOT THE
DIFFERENCES
DIFFƎRƎNCƎS

John Baptist de la Salle started two schools, but they don't look the same. Circle the 6 differences.

WORD SEARCH

```
D C F S C H O O L K
H R O T N E M G J E
Y L A R D E H T A C
R S G I W Z K E B N
A P Z W V N K O O A
N O R E D N U O F R
I O Q S M U L S Y F
M R E H C A E T G N
E O R T O I N V H I
S N E R D L I H C L
```

Find these 10 words! The words can be straight across, backward, up, or down.

WORD BANK

CATHEDRAL	POOR
CHILDREN	SCHOOL
FOUNDER	SEMINARY
FRANCE	SLUMS
MENTOR	TEACHER

Tracing Time

The Christian Brothers lived Jesus' words: *"Whoever does the will of God is my brother and sister and mother"* (Mark 3:35).

Practice tracing the letters of the word *"BROTHERS."*

B B B
R R R
O O O
T T T
H H H
E E E
R R R
S S S

PACK THE BACKPACK

Help this student get ready for **school**.
Circle the items that belong in the backpack.

SCRAMBLED PRAYER

Unscramble the CAPITALIZED words to complete the "Glory Be" (Doxology).

LOYRG be to the RAFETH,

_____   _____

and to the ONS, and to the

_____

YOHL spirit, as it was in the

_____

INNENGGIB, is now, and ever

_____

shall be, DROWL without end.

_____

NAEM.

FIND the HIDDEN ANIMALS

IN THE GARDEN

When Joan was a little girl, she helped her parents in the garden. Draw your garden in the space below, using flowers, fruits, vegetables, or any plant you lik

MAZE

Help Joan find her way
to the castle so Charles can be crowned king!

WORD SEARCH

```
B R A V E Q M K O Z
S G Z R S L Z N E E
T H E O L O G I A N
B P S M I E R G J K
A F P Z U F T H U R
N Q A N C A S T L E
N I E A R M O R C G
E C O M M A N D E R
R T N E C O N N I F
G A S D L E I H S I
```

Find these 10 words! The words can be straight across, backward, up, or down.

ARMOR	INNOCENT
BANNER	KNIGHT
BRAVE	REIMS
CASTLE	SHIELD
COMMANDER	THEOLOGIAN

Memorare Prayer

Like Joan, we can pray to Mary when we need help. Complete the prayer below by filling in the blanks with the missing words from the word bank.

_____, O most gracious _____ Mary, that never was it known that anyone who fled to thy protection, implored thy help, or sought thine _____ was left _____. Inspired by this _____, I fly unto thee. O Virgin of virgins, my _____ ; to thee do I come, before thee I stand, sinful and _____. O Mother of the _____ Incarnate, despise not my _____, but in thy mercy hear and answer me.

Amen.

WORD BANK

confidence	intercession	mother
Remember	sorrowful	Word
petitions	unaided	Virgin

SUITING UP

Draw a line from the object or piece of armor to the place it belongs on the soldier's body.

COLLECTING TAXES

Add or subtract the coins and write the answer.

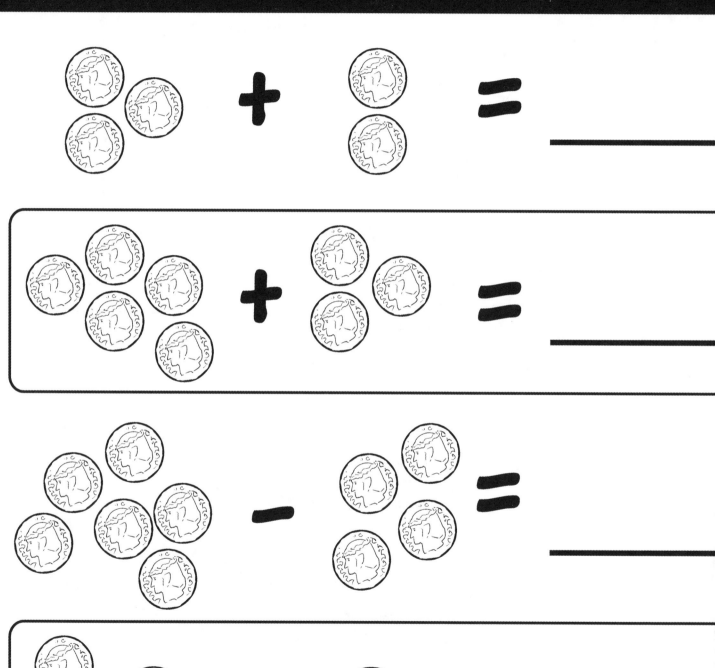

SETTING THE TABLE

Matthew invited some friends to dinner. If **you** invited **your** friends to dinner, circle what you would need to set the table, then draw the feast **food and all!**

Tracing Time

Matthew wrote one of the Gospels in the Bible. Now you can write "Matthew's Gospel" by tracing the letters below.

Matthew's Gospel

Matthew's Gospel

Matthew's Gospel

 WROTE THE BIBLE?

The names of the authors of the four Gospels are found below. Find and circle them.

Mark

Paul

John

George

Justin

Luke

Peter

Matthew

WORD SEARCH

```
B L Y R O I V A S O
A D T H E R U F S T
N D D A A Y J F J S
K J I E L C A R I M
E S S F W D M M J L
R E C O I N S O E F
A X I U E X Y N S D
Z A P O S T L E U M
O T L G P Y L Y S Q
M H E C M A R T Y R
```

Find these 10 words! The words can be
straight across, backward, up, or down.

WORD BANK

APOSTLE	MARTYR
BANKER	MIRACLE
COINS	MONEY
DISCIPLE	SAVIOR
JESUS	TAXES

Help Jesus reach Lazarus in the tomb by finding the correct path through the maze.

15

13

14

3

12

5

11

4

10

9

DOT
·TO·
DOT

8

6

7

DRAW SAINT THOMAS

Copy what you see in each small square onto the matching large square.

BUILDING THE CHURCH

Design a church like Thomas by decorating the building below with steeple, windows, statues, shapes, and anything you and God like.

WORD JUMBLE

These words are all mixed up!
Can you unscramble them?

LTEWE   _____

BOTUD   _____

EVLIEBE   _____

RGUACEO   _____

RASEPI   _____

OMNSISRAIY   _____

HRECTICAT   _____

WORD BANK

BELIEVE
MISSIONARY
TWELVE
COURAGE
ARCHITECT
PERSIA
DOUBT

THOMAS SPEAKS

The words of Saint Thomas are found in John's Gospel. Fill in the blanks to complete the verses using the word bank to help you.

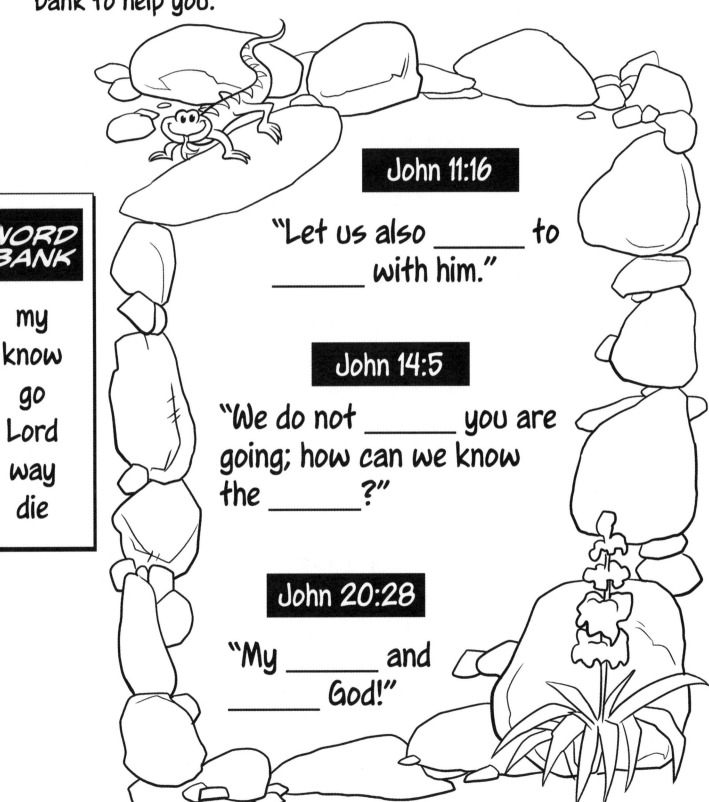

WORD BANK

my
know
go
Lord
way
die

John 11:16

"Let us also _____ to _____ with him."

John 14:5

"We do not _____ you are going; how can we know the _____?"

John 20:28

"My _____ and _____ God!"

SPOT THE
DIFFERENCES
DIFFƎRƎNCƎS

These two pictures of the risen Jesus aren't quite the same. Can you find 6 differences?

COMMUNITY
ROLES

Draw a line to connect the workers with the places they serve.

SPREADING THE FAITH

Number the people below in the order in which they came to the Christian faith.

ROCK BAND

Let's start a band! Circle the objects
you need from the items below.

LOVE SONG

Write a letter, poem, or song lyrics that tell Jesus how much you love him!

DRAW SAINT
CECILIA

Copy what you see in each
small square onto the
matching large square.

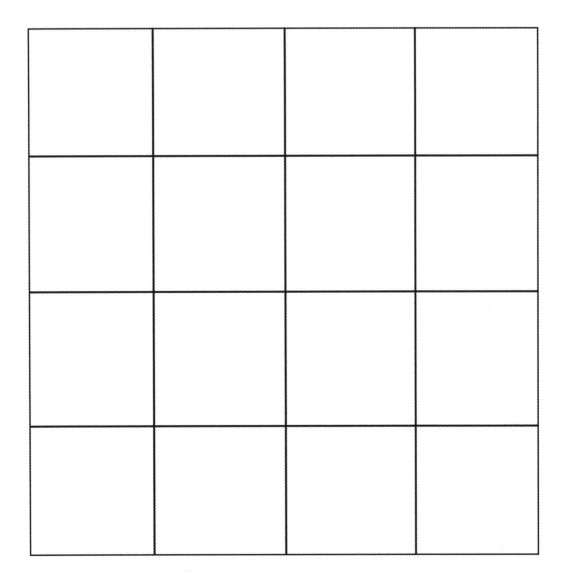

TIC-TAC-TOE

Play with
a friend! Put X's or O's
in the paving stones.

WORD SEARCH

```
D T N Y P E P I L D
S E A H B G Q T C J
C N I N E V A E H V
I S C U L P T U R E
A P I H S R O W I F
S O S V C C F O S A
O X U N A M O R T I
M A M M U X Z A I T
Q A I L I C E C A H
E V A L E R I A N I
```

Find these 10 words! The words can be
straight across, backward, up, or down.

WORD BANK

CECILIA
CHRISTIAN
FAITH
HEAVEN
MOSAIC

MUSICIAN
ROMAN
SCULPTURE
VALERIAN
WORSHIP

PRINCE OF ANGELS

Decorate Saint Michael's crown and shield.

WORD JUMBLE

These words are all mixed up!
Can you unscramble them?

FEDDEN   _____

LIHACEM   _____

TORPCET   _____

VEANHE   _____

SINERH   _____

GARLACHNE   _____

FULCERI   _____

WORD BANK

ARCHANGEL
HEAVEN
LUCIFER
SHRINE
DEFEND
PROTECT
MICHAEL

Saint Michael Prayer

Let's pray the prayer to Saint Michael! Complete the prayer by filling in the blanks with the missing words from the word bank.

Saint Michael the _____, defend us in _____. Be our _____ against the _____ and snares of the Devil. May God _____ him, we humbly pray, and do thou, O Prince of the _____ hosts, by the power of God, thrust into _____ _____ and all the evil spirits who prowl about the world seeking the ruin of souls.

Amen.

WORD BANK

Archangel	defense
Satan	rebuke
battle	hell
heavenly	wickedness

SPOT THE
DIFFERENCES
DIFFƎRƎNCƎS

These two angels aren't quite the same. Can you find 6 differences between them?

MAZE

God sent Lucifer to hell. With Saint Michael, show him the way.

DRAW THE
AMBULANCE

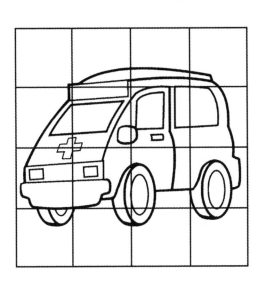

Copy what you see in each
small square onto the
matching large square.

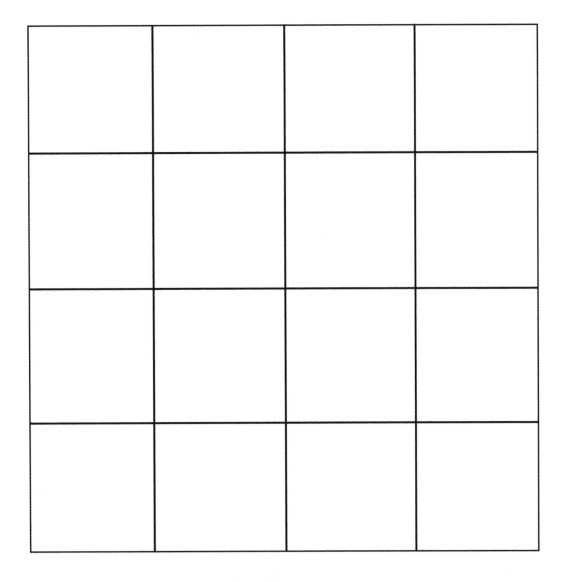

SPOT THE DIFFERENCES

John Baptist de la Salle started two schools, but they don't look the same. Circle the 6 differences.

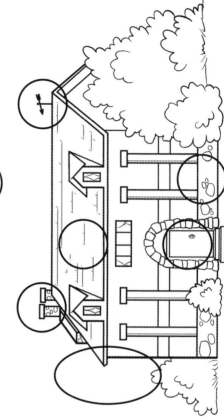

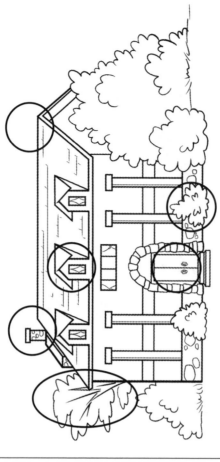

HIDDEN OBJECTS

This Lasallian teacher is missing a few school supplies. Circle the items listed.

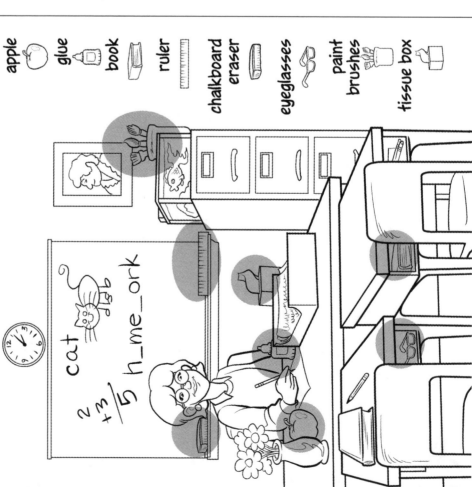

apple

glue

book

ruler

chalkboard eraser

eyeglasses

paint brushes

tissue box

cat

2
+3
/5 h_me_ork

PACK THE BACKPACK

Help this student get ready for school.
Circle the items that belong in the backpack.

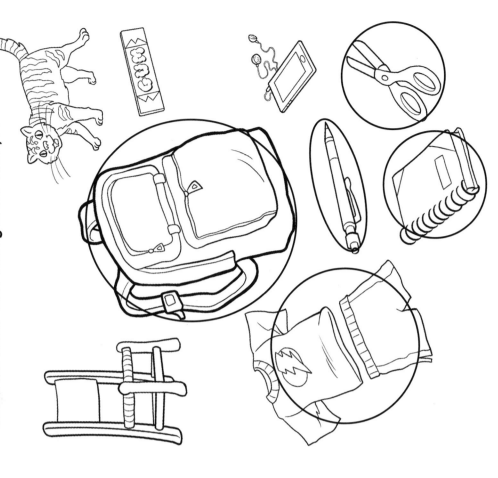

WORD SEARCH

```
D C F S C H O O L K
H R O T N E M G J E
Y L A R D E H T A C
R S G I W Z K E B N
A P Z W V N K O O A
N O R E D N U O F R
I O Q S M U L S Y F
M R E H C A E T G N
E O R T O I N V H I
S N E R D L I H C L
```

Find these 10 words! The words can be straight across, backward, up, or down.

WORD BANK

CATHEDRAL   POOR
CHILDREN   SCHOOL
FOUNDER   SEMINARY
FRANCE   SLUMS
MENTOR   TEACHER

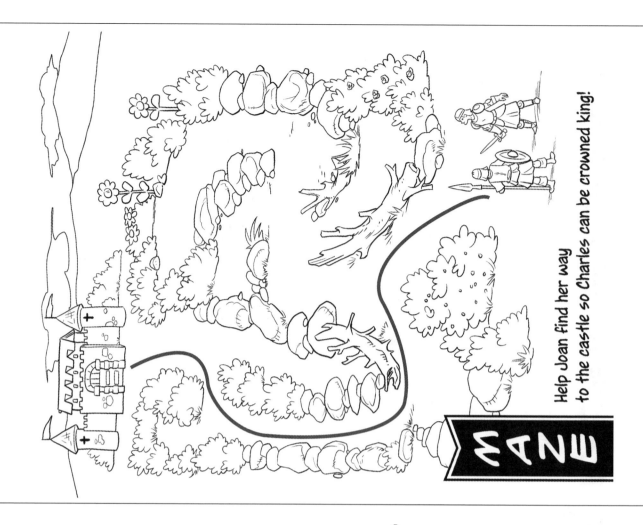

MAZE

Help Joan find her way to the castle so Charles can be crowned king!

SCRAMBLED PRAYER

Unscramble the CAPITALIZED words to complete the "Glory Be" (Doxology).

LOYRG be to the **RAFETH,**
GLORY   FATHER

and to the **ONS,** and to the
SON

YOHL spirit, as it was in the
HOLY

INNENGGIB, is now, and ever
BEGINNING

shall be, **DROWL** without end.
WORLD

NAEM.
AMEN

Memorare Prayer

Like Joan, we can pray to Mary when we need help. Complete the prayer below by filling in the blanks with the missing words from the word bank.

Remember, O most gracious Virgin Mary, that never was it known that anyone who fled to thy protection, implored thy help, or sought thine intercession was left unaided. Inspired by this confidence, I fly unto thee. O Virgin of virgins, my mother; to thee do I come, before thee I stand, sinful and sorrowful. O Mother of the Word Incarnate, despise not my petitions, but in thy mercy hear and answer me.

Amen.

WORDSEARCH

```
B R A V E Q M K O Z
S G Z R S L Z N E E
T H E O L O G I A N
B P S M I E R G J K
A F P Z U F T H U R
Q A N C A S T L E
N I E A R M O R C G
E C O M M A N D E R
R T N E C O N N I F
G A S D L E I H S I
```

Find these 10 words! The words can be straight across, backward, up, or down.

COLLECTING TAXES

Add or subtract the coins and write the answer.

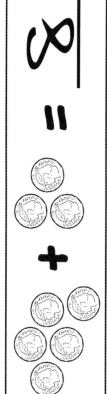 +  = 5 ___

 +  = 8 ___

 -  = 2 ___

 -  = 3 ___

SUITING UP

Draw a line from the object or piece of armor to the place it belongs on the soldier's body.

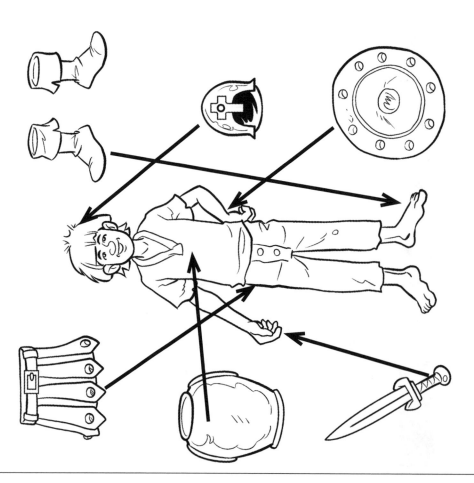

WHO WROTE THE BIBLE?

The names of the authors of the four Gospels are found below. Find and circle them.

John

Luke

Matthew

Paul

Justin

Peter

Mark

George

SETTING THE TABLE

Matthew invited some friends to dinner. If you invited your friends to dinner, circle what you would need to set the table, then draw the feast — food and all!

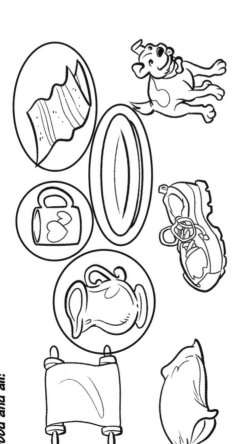

MAZE

Help Jesus reach Lazarus in the tomb by finding the correct path through the maze.

WORD SEARCH

```
B L Y R O I V A S O
A T H E R U F S T
N D D A A Y J F J S
K J I E L C A R I M
E S S F W D M J L
R E C O I N S O E F
A X I U E X Y N S D
Z A P O S T L E U M
O T L G P Y L Y S Q
M H E C M A R T Y R
```

Find these 10 words! The words can be straight across, backward, up, or down.

WORD BANK

APOSTLE
BANKER
COINS
DISCIPLE
JESUS

MARTYR
MIRACLE
MONEY
SAVIOR
TAXES

WORD JUMBLE

These words are all mixed up!
Can you unscramble them?

TWELVE

DOUBT

BELIEVE

COURAGE

PERSIA

MISSIONARY

ARCHITECT

LTEWE

BOTUD

EVLIEBE

RGUACEO

RASEPI

OMNSISRAIY

HRECTICAT

WORD BANK

BELIEVE
MISSIONARY
TWELVE
COURAGE
ARCHITECT
PERSIA
DOUBT

Connect the dots to finish the picture.

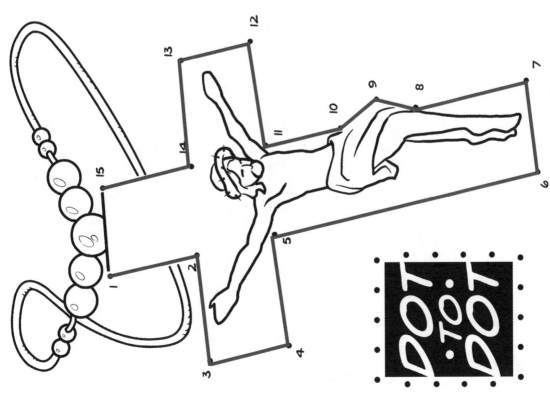

DOT · TO · DOT

SPOT THE DIFFERENCES

These two pictures of the risen Jesus aren't quite the same. Can you find 6 differences?

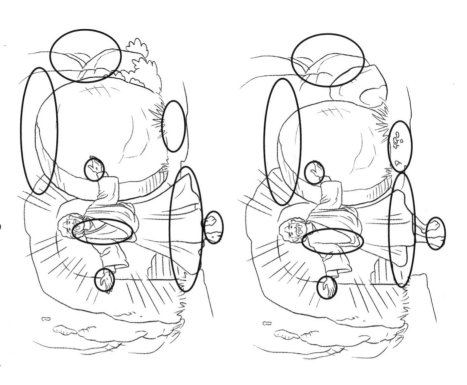

THOMAS SPEAKS

The words of Saint Thomas are found in John's Gospel. Fill in the blanks to complete the verses using the word bank to help you.

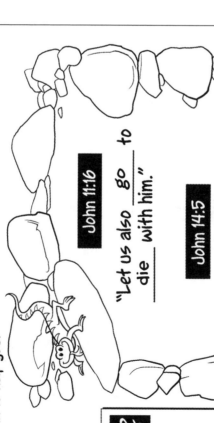

John 11:16

"Let us also _go_ _to_ _die_ with him."

John 14:5

"We do not _know_ you are going; how can we know the _way_ ?"

John 20:28

"My _Lord_ and my _God_!"

WORD BANK

my
know
go
Lord
way
die

SPREADING THE FAITH

Number the people below in the order in which they came to the Christian Faith.

COMMUNITY ROLES

Draw a line to connect the workers with the places they serve.

WORD SEARCH

D T N Y P E P I L D
S E A H B G Q T C J
C N I N E V A E H V
I S C U L P T U R E
A P I H S R O W I F
S O S V C C F O S A
O X U N A M O R T I
M A M U X Z A I T H
Q A L I C E C A H
E V A L E R I A N I

Find these 10 words! The words can be straight across, backward, up, or down.

WORD BANK

CECILIA	MUSICIAN
CHRISTIAN	ROMAN
FAITH	SCULPTURE
HEAVEN	VALERIAN
MOSAIC	WORSHIP

ROCK BAND

Let's start a band! Circle the objects you need from the items below.

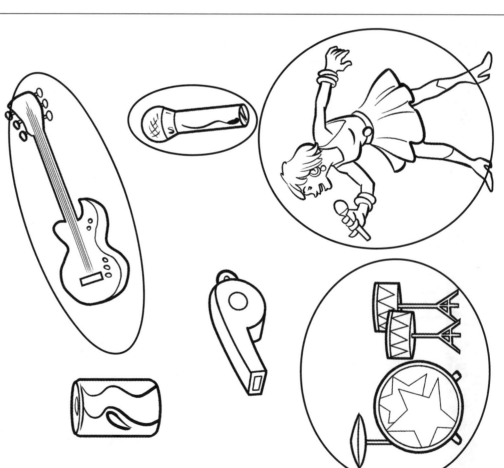

Saint Michael Prayer

Let's pray the prayer to Saint Michael! Complete the prayer by filling in the blanks with the missing words from the word bank.

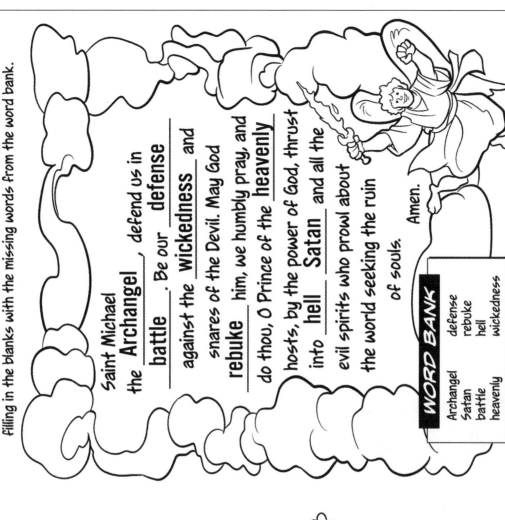

Saint Michael the **Archangel**, defend us in **battle**. Be our **defense** against the **wickedness** and snares of the Devil. May God **rebuke** him, we humbly pray, and do thou, O Prince of the **heavenly** hosts, by the power of God, thrust into **hell** **Satan** and all the evil spirits who prowl about the world seeking the ruin of souls. Amen.

WORD BANK

Archangel	defense
Satan	rebuke
battle	hell
heavenly	wickedness

WORD JUMBLE

These words are all mixed up! Can you unscramble them?

FEDDEN   DEFEND

LIHACEM   MICHAEL

TORPCET   PROTECT

VEANHE   HEAVEN

SINERH   SHRINE

GARLACHNE   ARCHANGEL

FULCERI   LUCIFER

WORD BANK

ARCHANGEL
HEAVEN
LUCIFER
SHRINE
DEFEND
PROTECT
MICHAEL

MAZE

God sent Lucifer to hell. With Saint Michael, show him the way.

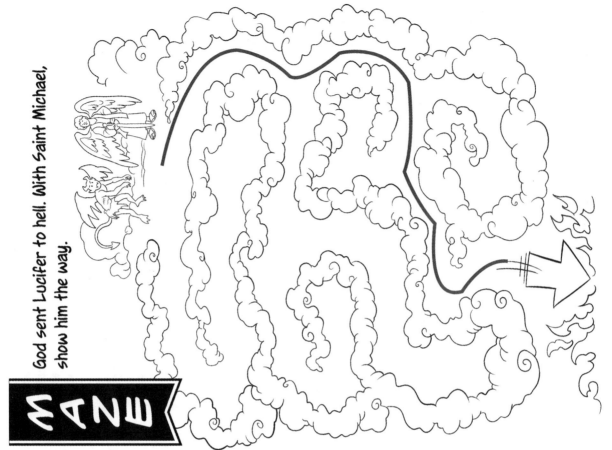

SPOT THE DIFFERENCES

These two angels aren't quite the same. Can you find 6 differences between them?

saints and me! series

saints for communities

John Baptist de la Salle: Caring Teacher and Mentor

Joan of Arc: Brave Soldier for Peace

Matthew the Apostle: Banker and God's Storyteller

Cecilia: Singing and Sharing the Faith

Michael the Archangel: Protector of God's People

Thomas the Apostle: Builder and Believer

Saints for Communities Activity Book

saints of christmas

Nicholas of Myra: Giver of Many Gifts

Francis of Assisi: Keeper of Creation

Martin de Porres: A Beggar for Justice

Gianna Beretta Molla: Wife, Mother, and Doctor

Mary and Joseph: Models of Faith and Love

Lucy: A Light for Jesus

Saints of Christmas Activity Book

saints of north America

Kateri Tekakwitha: Model of Bravery

Juan Diego: Mary's Humble Messenger

Elizabeth Ann Seton: Mother for Many

André Bessette: A Heart of Strength

Rose Philippine Duchesne: A Dreamer and a° Missionary

Damien of Molokai: Builder of Community

Saints of North America Activity Book

saints for families

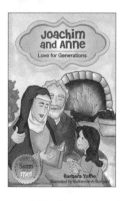

Anthony of Padua: Wonder Worker

John Bosco: Champion for Youth

Thérèse of Lisieux: Little Flower of Love

Gerard Majella: Guardian of Mothers

Joachim and Anne: Love for Generations

Thomas More: Faith-Filled Father

Saints for Families Activity Book

About the Author

Jeff Albrecht has illustrated for Disney, Warner Bros., Marvel, DC Comics, and other entertainment companies. His animation work has been seen on Cartoon Network. His Christian illustration credits include Master Books (A is for Adam, D is for Dinosaurs, N is for Noah), Bayard Inc. (Living Faith Kids), and Concordia Publishing House (Family Time). He enjoys working with different illustration styles from his studio in the St. Louis area.